small things left behind

small   things

ella zeltserman

left   behind

 The University of Alberta Press

Published by

The University of Alberta Press
Ring House 2
Edmonton, Alberta, Canada T6G 2E1
www.uap.ualberta.ca

LIBRARY AND ARCHIVES CANADA
CATALOGUING IN PUBLICATION

Zeltserman, Ella, 1955–, author
    Small things left behind / Ella
Zeltserman.

(Robert Kroetsch series)
Poems.
Issued in print and electronic formats.
ISBN 978-1-77212-002-8 (pbk.). —
ISBN 978-1-77212-012-7 (epub).—
ISBN 978-1-77212-013-4 (Amazon kindle). —
ISBN 978-1-77212-014-1 (pdf)

    I. Title. II. Series: Robert Kroetsch series

PS8649.E52S63 2014   C811'.6   C2014-904329-5
                          C2014-904330-9

First edition, first printing, 2014.
Printed and bound in Canada by Houghton
Boston Printers, Saskatoon, Saskatchewan.
Copyediting and proofreading by
Peter Midgley.

A volume in the Robert Kroetsch series.

The University of Alberta Press is committed
to protecting our natural environment.
As part of our efforts, this book is printed
on Enviro Paper: it contains 100% post-
consumer recycled fibres and is acid- and
chlorine-free.

The University of Alberta Press gratefully
acknowledges the support received for
its publishing program from The Canada
Council for the Arts. The University of
Alberta Press also gratefully acknowledges
the financial support of the Government of
Canada through the Canada Book Fund (CBF)
and the Government of Alberta through
the Alberta Multimedia Development Fund
(AMDF) for its publishing activities.

For Mark and Lea who made that journey with me
For Jacob who was born into freedom
For Malka and Constance who inherit these family stories

In memory of my mother Maria Lubotskaya

contents

I was born at the right time
in the history of the Soviet Union.
I missed being among millions
dead in Gulag camps.
I missed being thrown out
of cattle cars into the Siberian snow
in the summer dress
I wore on the day of my arrest.

I missed being shot
in blood-stained prison basements,
having my remains dumped
into an unmarked grave.
I missed knocks on the door
the middle of night
Black Marusia snatching me
from life.

I missed being swollen from hunger
and dying during the Ukrainian famine.
I missed being robbed of my lands and possessions.
I was born after Stalin's death.
I grew up during Brezhnev's vegetarian times.
I was so lucky. I missed.
I missed.
But I knew and I feared.

* *Black Marusia*—Black car used by KGB during arrests from the 1930s to 1950s

let my people go

1 | the documentary

Thunderstorm in the winter.
Revelation from God on Mount Sinai.
On the screen—a Jewish couple
believing in Zion   they emigrate to Israel.

Disillusioned, poor and sick, they come back
disembark from the train
drop on their knees
kiss the homeland.

I fly from the theatre holding my breath.
It is possible to leave this Soviet prison.
I forget the rest of the movie.

2 | old Polly

Rumours float, in whispers.
At my school the teacher of theoretical mechanics leaves.
She is declared a traitor and a parasite
she is dragged through the mud
spat at   by her colleagues.
Later, the most vehement accusers themselves leave.

Old Polly, prematurely grey
washed out
scared—nonentity
surprises me by the smile on her face and in her eyes
as though somebody has given her back
twenty years of life and a future.

3 | let my people eat

The dream, the unbelievable,
the impossible becomes possible.
Risk everything
have some guts, some luck
and an invitation
from non-existent relatives in Israel.
The KGB pharaohs know about the non-existence—
experts in the cat and mouse game.

Very noisy LET MY PEOPLE GO campaign.
Thousands of strangers worldwide
march for our freedom
in front of the Soviet consulates.
In the end "the Party" sells us.
LET MY PEOPLE EAT.

We are the payment
for the bushels of wheat.

* the Party—the Communist Party of the USSR

release

I was not present when my parents signed my release papers.
Told them the date I needed the papers back
walked out of the apartment.
Out of their lives.

Just another round of signature-gathering.
I left the papers with them in their kitchen.
White stove, white furniture, shiny-brown linoleum floor
and the yeasty smell of freshly baked pies.

I did not hear their whispered conversation,
their hollow voices devoid of life.
I did not see my mother's tears
as she got the pen to sign under her lonely years.

I did not smell the air heavy with despair
as my father put the papers back into the envelope.
Did not taste the tea my mother made later that evening.
The tea of bitter sleepless nights before her.

I did not touch their hands
cold as corpses' hands
as they sat holding each other
in the suddenly empty apartment. In the dark.

I came to pick up the papers.
Looked at the signatures.
All was in order.
My parents' quiet voices.

The home smelled of a dead body.
Nobody mentioned the coffin
in the middle of the room.
Nobody had the strength to move.

end of my life in a box

There is a box full of my life neatly fitted in.
My brother starts the fire in the water tank
in the bathroom. He throws in the photographs
of my friends in underwear and ties, two of them,
one short, one tall. One dark, one blond, two
class clowns who played off each other.
Love poems from one of them, love letters
from the other and lots of messages
passed under school desks. My notebooks
full of copied poems from my favourite poets,
about love. More photographs, more letters.
The years up in flames.
Real love, real pain—into the fire.
My brother sweating. The water boiling.
Me?   Leaving.

not scared

I don't have any fear of leaving left.
I am excited about the future
Vienna, Rome
crossing the border

so unattainable
words I never dreamed.
Out of prison
out, out

into a wide world.
I am not scared, I dance.
My father is scared
he worries

about us dying from hunger
on capitalist streets—
propaganda he sees
on daily Soviet newsreels

always disaster in the capitalist countries
always blooming gardens in the socialist ones.

My husband laughs.
I am an engineer
I don't think I can be as poor anywhere else
as I am here.

Nothing to lose
except prison walls
fear, constant lies
buried thoughts.

Freedom is something my father has never known.
How do I explain freedom to the ones born bent?

baggage

Lenin, the great creator
looks at us from the dirty old frame
on the grey wall of the customs office.
Customs decides
what we can or cannot take. They pack and ship.
We do not have any lumber to make your crate
says the Customs Official. He does not hate us.
It is a simple fact.
The phrase "We do not have"
is as common as "Ahead to the Victory of Communism!"
on the TV, the radio, in every newspaper, and every school book.
It is this victory we are running from.

We look at each other
back at the official.
When?

"Well." He takes a piece of paper from the pile on his desk.
"I will have the lumber by July thirtieth.
Bring your stuff on August tenth."
We have the tickets to leave on August fifth.
"Well, you can change your tickets."
He has finished with us.

On a July morning in Leningrad
we stand in the middle of the Soviet reality
surrounded by unseen barbed wire.
Habitual fear hunches my shoulders,

bends my head down
in a gust of cold wind from the Baltic.
A quick knowing glance at my husband's Jewish nose from a passerby.
The sound of cheerful victory music from a nearby window.
Run, run, run.

My father comes to see us in the evening.
How did it go with the luggage?
It did not. We will leave it behind.
Lumber? my father repeats, lumber I can find.
Next day the plant where he works delivers
a trainload of lumber to the customs office
so they can make one small crate for us.
We leave on the fifth.

It takes a year for the crate to reach us in Edmonton.
The thick steel plates of my knitting machine
have been bent with a heavy tool.
They hated us after all.
And our daughter's crib?
She already has a new one.
Out come bed linens, a few pots and pans
heavy dictionaries and reference books
a volume of Pushkin's poems.

We chopped up the precious lumber.
Threw it into the garbage.

last visit at my parents' home

We walk in
Our daughter runs to kiss us
Hugs   commotion
So many people in a small entrance hall
Nobody says anything

The photographer comes
Sit here   move there   now the three of you
Everybody—smile
I will have pictures ready tomorrow
Nobody says anything

We have dinner
The whole family at the table
Noise
Animated discussions
Everybody drinks to our future

We are at the door   goodbye kisses
All of a sudden   my mother gets pale
—You are never coming home again—
She drops into a chair like a wounded bird
Hands to her mouth   catching the words

I silently nod
Close the door behind me
Without a sound

We are allowed five suitcases to pack all our lives into
and deliver to the customs office at the airport, five days before
our flight to Vienna, so the KGB can rummage through

the remains of our past that we're taking into the future,
away from the foreigners' eyes. Hours to ponder each piece,
read each line, look at each photo. What do they search for

in the old family letters? Why can't I take
my mother's picture, if she wrote a date or her name on it?
Unfathomable. We stop even trying to understand.

A young KGB officer reads the correspondence between
my husband and his late father. Half an hour later
he makes a vile remark, looks at my husband, contempt

in his eyes, says—you cannot take them. Finality
in his voice. Why not? His reply—I have to read
each one, and I don't want to. My husband gets tense.

I have the right to take them—you must read them. Rights!
I am scared of the word. You do not cross a KGB officer
no matter what. He can do any evil he wants to us.

My husband cannot give up. These letters are all that is left
from his father. The room starts to look like a prison cell—
walls, no windows, guards. At this moment a superior,
a Major, walks in. What's the matter? Our tormentor points

at the open suitcase. The Major peers at my husband—squared
jaw and tight fists, picks up a few photographs. Half whisper,

Your father fought in the war. Turns to the junior—Put the letters
back into a suitcase and let it go. You heard me, they can have them.
The Major's hair is grey. There is a scar on his cheek.

My little daughter holds her teddy bear, dirty, old, yellow Mishka, as she crosses the airport gate. They are best friends. He helped us a lot already today, when the two of us stood at five in the morning on an empty patch of green in the middle of the ochre-coloured stone jungle of Leningrad.

We take the cab to the airport at dawn. The city starts to wake up. Empty streets. Cold northern sun glides on the mirror of the steel canals reflected in my heart. Your sudden voice—stop the car, I forgot our tickets and documents—your face now white like your mother's hair. Words fall like snow in the middle of summer. Terror runs down my spine. We can leave only once. We signed the papers to be out of the country. If we don't leave, we will all go to jail. The end of our lives flashes in front of my eyes. I freeze, the winds of Siberia on my mind.

The puzzled driver turns the car around. Back to our friends' empty apartment, where we spent our last night at home. Our baby daughter cannot take that much. She gets carsick. Stop the car. Two of us step out, three—teddy goes with us. The car speeds away. We are nowhere.

I tell a story to my little child and her friend Mishka, as we sit, cuddled. I hug my daughter, she hugs the teddy, and the fear tightly hugs us—on one bench. Not a soul in sight. I pray there will be no militia car driving by. I pray the cab does not crash. I pray you find the key to the apartment. I pray and I pray for you to come back. I feel forsaken in this city, suddenly not at all mine. I keep the fairytale going, check the teddy. He looks fine, my daughter keeps up with him.

The car comes back; we get in. The city zooms past, no show of love. I am reeling. Our child gets sick. Stop the car, her grandmother cries. Desperate. The voice of an old woman who has already lost all. Keep going, keep going. It is our last chance. The child throws up on the floor. The driver gets angry. Two hundred, my husband says, sets the pack of now useless rubles in front of his eyes. The driver nods. The car shoots out—a bullet, an arrow carrying us to a new life.

We've made it. Run toward the gates. The cries of our family— drops of blood from broken hearts. Last touches and hugs. We go through customs, more malicious questions, about one piece of silver, one spoon left from my husband's grandmother. A river of tears runs through me into the sea of sorrows surrounding us. Dear faces never to be seen again. But our motherland worries about a spoon, a ring, a photograph of my father in a military uniform. There are no human beings here, only *Homo soveticus* machines.

The door to freedom is right there.   We can see it.
Just let us out.   Let us go   across this line!

It is over. The big glass wall separates us. We've walked to the other side. Only the three of us—and the teddy, dirty old Mishka.

I cannot ever heal the pain of that moment
Our family cried, forlorn, desolate, lost to us

Tortured faces sandblasted on glass
For the remaining years of our lives

Only the three of us
Checked in on the flight to Vienna

It hurts when the birds cry
I hear my mother echoing them

airborne

At the bottom of the stairs to the plane, the young flight
attendant looks at my husband and he at her. They know each
other, they met once a week for two years at the State English
courses that have paved their way to their futures. Welcome,
please enjoy your flight, only words exchanged. The trained
smile—she does not blink, neither does he. Her job is at stake.
His life.

Dinner is served at the beginning of the flight, caviar and
champagne. The show goes on unchanged—let the world know,
we are the country where even ordinary people eat caviar. The
murmur passes between emigrant families (there are eight on
the plane): save the champagne for crossing the border, when
we lose our Soviet citizenship, become refugees. An hour later
the pilot announces in a solemn voice full of importance, we
have crossed the border of the USSR. The loud Hurrahs from one
end of the plane to another, the stares from the other startled
passengers. We are airborne. It is an international flight. The
plane cannot turn back.

My husband recites Lermontov, loud.

> Farewell dirty Russia
> The country of slaves
> The country of masters
> And you, blue uniforms
> And you, people obedient to them
> Perhaps behind the wall of Caucasus

          I will get rid at last
          Of your all-seeing eye
          And your all-hearing ear.

The verses, more than hundred years old, speak to us. We drink.
We say FREEDOM from one to another, along the rows of seats.

I look through the window, down, down, as if I expect to see the
iron wall reaching up to the plane. There is none. Just clouds,
more clouds, patches of sky and us, as we soar above, moving
further and further, away from the blue uniforms.

---

* Lermontov—a well-known 19th-century Russian poet

August 5th 1979

My daughter jumps with joy, no care in the world
in a little square across from the hotel
where charity officials sort us like dirty laundry.
She plays under a blue sky on a sunny summer day
in Vienna.
As if she did not just cross the iron curtain
separating two worlds.
As if she did not leave everything behind.
All her toys in the empty apartment
and the grandparents she will not see again.
She jumps like there is no boogieman in her life.
But there was one, an hour ago
as we stepped from the plane and walked into the building.
Aliens landing on an unknown planet
a small group   stunned, blinded.
Refugees.
All of a sudden she runs to this big, tall Austrian guard
blond hair, blue eyes, leather jacket and a submachine gun.
Straight from the movies about Nazis or a capitalist hell.
My heart freezes, I am unable to cry.
I scream without a sound coming from me.
My child!
And as if I watch a slow motion movie
I see   he smiles, picks her up and tosses her into the air.
She laughs, both of them laugh.
Pearls of their laughter hit the big glass door
through which we've been born
into this forbidden, intimidating world.

The submachine gun dangles, hits his knees.
More laughter, more tosses.
Everybody—speechless
as we watch a whole pack of lies tumbling down
in big chunks of iron.

torn. gone.

We had only two shirts for you when we left, the one you were wearing and the one in the suitcase, and two bars of soap.

We had the instructions typed on some old typewriter and handed, clandestinely, from one emigrant to another. (We were not emigrants yet. We were "leaving" for family and friends. "Traitors. Parasites. Enemies. Dirty Jews," for everybody else.)

KGB-defying Jews, experienced in *Samizdat*, compiled the advice, sent back by the daring souls who had already left. By the time we were packing in 1979, we had a complete manual. It explained—all stores in Vienna were closed from Saturday noon to Monday morning, the plane from Leningrad arrived on Saturday—better pack enough food to last for two days, some soap, and laundry detergent. (I said, if we have to take that, why are we going?) Detergent we did not take. About the pots and pans, where to sell one hundred grams of caviar, two bottles of vodka and one of champagne. Regardless of how much life you left behind—a hundred rubles per person was all you could take.

We left—stripped of everything.
Possessions Illusions Identity Friends Family Home
with only two pieces of soap.

You left one the first time you took a shower in a pension. Immediately you ran back—the soap, the soap. It was gone. Next day the same. After the last bar was lost, we sat in our room. Outraged. Horrified. Who could have done such an abominable deed? How are we going to afford to buy another one? Then— you tried to open the window, got your sleeve caught on the latch. TRRRRRRRRRRR. We looked at each other, in panic and—laughed.   We were   free.

* *Samizdat*—underground publishing of texts forbidden in the Soviet Union

crowds

Smiles on people's faces are unusual to see.
On the streets of Leningrad people do not smile.
They look glum and grey.

Here, people walk straighter
free and sure of themselves
they hurry around on the orderly streets of Vienna.

Their clothes are bright.
Old women elegantly dressed.
The way passersby look into my eyes.

Is it possible to live without fear?

déjà vu

Time and again, when I think about that trip, I see the same picture. An empty platform, an SS man stands next to the train in full uniform, black boots and black leather gloves.

We were told to go to a station at night. Find the train without a number on platform such and such. Don't miss it, there will be no announcement. We went to some kind of *bahnhof*. The train was there—no sign, no light (precautions against terrorist attack). We found an empty compartment, our friends got the next. An older man came and asked to join us. The train was full when it left.

We moved in the darkness. We took seats, put our daughter to sleep. I felt my husband's body and held my little girl's hand as the train rolled along the terrain of my dread. I dozed off, opened my eyes to bright light. The train stopped. I looked through the window—fields, some trees on the horizon and everything emerald green. Fairytale country.

Commotion inside. Loud foreign voices along the hallway. A big, beefy man in all-black clothing walked into our berth. Towering over me he grabbed our suitcase. My heart dropped to my heels. I opened my mouth to scream—terrorists! And at the same time I saw his black eyes—smiling, kind. It all happened in a second. Next, he threw our suitcase out the window. Somebody outside caught it. My husband jumped up, threw another suitcase through the window. By that time, all along the train suitcases were flying, people were running.

The men motioned us out. Terrified, we boarded the buses waiting for us. Nothing happened. Except—the bright sun shone in the deep blue sky, the green welcoming earth was warm, music blasted, the young driver sang in Italian, we drove to Rome.

watermelon

We stayed in a little pension by *Termini*.
The noise of trains and police sirens
mixed up in our minds
with the cries of our parents
left behind
with the whisper of our souls
over the loss
with the rumblings of our stomachs
from the watery pasta we had every day.

One evening we went to the market
just before closing
when prices would be the lowest.
We bought one large watermelon,
shared the purchase with friends.
Proudly carried our catch to the room
looked at it with love and lust
and found we had no knife.

In desperation we dropped the treasure
on some crumpled suitcase-paper spread on the table.

The striped green cracked
and split into gorgeous pieces.
The pink sugary heaven, sparkling like stars
sent by the gods of the melon patch
filled the room
our mouths
dripped around and disappeared.
Gone as quickly as the night stars with the coming sun.

emigration

Is it a beehive?
Is it an anthill?
Is it a wasp nest?

A swarm of disoriented people
On a blob of stinking cow dung
Suspended in time

Wait their turn in the sorting game
Roll of a die—they are moved
Different fates for each one

Game is tormenting
Game is slow
Life is upside-down

You turn your skin inside-out
And swallow your personal spoonful
Of emigrant's shit

Ostia beach study with three lives
one month after escape

A shtetl's fear of water runs in your blood
Son of Berdichev's rabbis and Frankfurt's merchants.
You pensively dip your toe into the sea, just a touch.
That's it. That's enough.
You look apprehensively
into the sandy waters of the Tyrrhenian sea.
You like things to be clear.
You like to see things through.

This water colour does not impress me,
neither the deep blue of the Black Sea
nor the steel of my beloved icy Baltic.
I will never see them again.
Compromise is my life.
I walk into the brownish muck.
Murky like the memories
like the dreams of the lost home   no bottom to see.

Our baby daughter plays happily on the shore
splashes in the water, rolls in the sand.
The sun smiles at her.
She smiles at the world.
Water is just water.
Sand is just sand.
She has no thousand-year-old memories,
no life left behind.

I wake up in the middle of night

I don't remember:
Did I wipe the floor,
That last evening, before we left our trashed apartment?

Or did my mother, after they carried out our life's leftovers?
The sofa bed to be picked up by a neighbour
Three stools in our kitchen, the washing machine

And randomly-filled, opened boxes strewn around
It is easier to wash an empty floor.
I do not know.

What did my parents do after the plane left?
What did my mother say?
Where did they go?

Traditionally, there is a meal after the funeral.

you will be strangers in a strange land

We drink tea very late in the evening. Russian habits in the
midst of an Italian summer. The lamp over the table moves.
The floor shifts under our feet. The tremor I feel in my guts, a
split second of void in the middle of life. The tea spills from our
cups. We look through the window. A huge terrace prevents us
from observing the street. All over the building lights go on. We
run to the intercom, turn it on. We hear voices talking at once,
loud and fast. What is it? Disaster or carnival? The voices are
full of anxiety. I am pregnant with fright. We don't understand
a single word. I look into my husband's eyes. He looks at the
lamp. Listens to the intercom—it is an earthquake. I pause. Do
we take the baby and run? Wait. She may get scared. We listen
again to the artificial ear, our only link to the world. Everything
is quiet. Nobody runs. It is their country, they must know
better. We go back to the table. Sit through the night watching
the baby and the lamp. I cry. The night outside is warm, full of
sounds and smells we cannot comprehend.

perekati-pole

I stop dead.
Green sea under blue sky.
I drop on my knees
touch the grass.

Silky.
Luscious.
Smell of tranquility.

I've never seen grass as green
emerald green
in the middle of a scorching Roman August.

There is no such patch of grass
in my whole country.

The earth of my home
is ripped apart
blown up for most of its history.

We are children of the steppes whirled by wind.

* perekati-pole—tumbleweeds

Edmonton founded 1980

1| We landed in the city during a thaw, in February. Sun was
warm and everything around melted, the snow on the streets,
the houses and birds and people's faces. That January was
the coldest on record and City Hall had offered certificates to
those who needed confirmation of their endurance. We walked
along Jasper, people smiled at us, at the sun, they did not wear
hats and gloves, unzipped, unbuttoned, it did not feel like the
North at all. It did not feel like a city either, but a town with
cars and buses, small, low buildings and no bars. I needed
coffee, a small espresso, and we walked from block to block.
Bars were usually on corners, but here we found none, and the
word espresso did not appear in the vocabulary for another ten
years. I had to make do with my "Bialetti" in the morning and
without so many other things one takes for granted in a large
European city. This place had no people strolling downtown in
the evening, no promenade along the river, nobody ate or drank
at little tables along the streets. My eyes were hurt by staring at
building after building without character, by miles and miles
of greyish houses in suburbs, by riverbanks without granite, by
people's clothing, by the dryness of the air. Nothing in this city
talked to me, my soul was as empty as its streets and smells. I
had to twist myself into the pretzel that I went to hunt for in
German bakeries, which still had German bakers at the time,
and smelled faintly of Europe—an unreachable dream without
shape across the ocean.

Corners in the Pan American motel room were sharp. They
defined the shape of this new world in which we had been

dropped. We had to learn to speak, to work, to smile, to live and to make a home from the shreds of our past life and from gratitude to fate, for landing us here. That first morning we crossed the street to a small drugstore to buy toothpaste in English.

2| It changes slowly. You learn to live with it—not love, but at first live. You learn about cold and snow, that there is often no spring, and that after winter the hot days come at once and everybody changes into shorts, and immediately the smell of BBQ permeates the neighbourhood. You learn to have a nonchalant attitude toward the thermometer. It does not matter what it says, you go to work, you drive, you are an Albertan. You learn to eat steak, say Hi to passersby and appreciate that people try to understand your crooked English, and slowly you find yourself part of them, at home, at one with open endless skies, with prairies, with time that moves along canola fields, wheat fields, pump jacks, badlands, foothills and the Rockies. You let time do its job, fill your lungs with the air of this unknown city, your ears with the sound of a foreign language, and your nostrils with the smell of a land you never imagined existed. Your eyes adjust, your heart starts beating to the rhythms of this new world. One day, while driving back to the city from afar, you say—sincerely—I am coming home.

These words startle you. You surprise yourself.

blue night

The snowbanks of my childhood were taller
I did not grow up
I've moved to the prairies
on the other side of the planet.
Not enough snow here for the dark blue nights
where the shining wet snow still creaks under my boots.

The moisture in the air makes everything soft
not a sharp edge in sight
the tops of the trees are round
the houses have no corners
and the street lights merge into sky
their yellow circles the eyes of the night.

Huge snowflakes, the size of silver coins
melt on my stuck-out tongue.
Misty stars look down on my small town
the sky so soft, so low
I stretch my hand and snatch one happy star.
Drop it into my pocket
as I spin along the blue road
my arms out, propelling me.

The smiling moon looks and winks her hazy eyes
lights the silvery shimmering arrow home.
A small yellow window.

My mother waits for me
the yeasty smell of her just-baked pies
tea is brewing
fire logs chat inside the old stove.

Warmth and happiness—heaven
fitting place for the star I let out of my sparkling pocket.
The star so bright I can see it from afar
from the prairie city years ahead
where I live now
dreaming of the past
smelling the snow and my mother's pies.

they still censor my life

My son is born into freedom.
A bright fall day, blue sky
gold leaves and a touch
of frost on the withered grass.
His first photograph travels
to the other side of the globe.

Behind the Iron Curtain
KGB fingers scrutinize the gloss.
Search
for the hidden thoughts
before allowing my parents to ponder
who their grandson resembles.

the finger

My mother—the beggar.
Goes from one office to another.
The fat finger waves in front of her nose.
You will never see them.

Never.

The absolute certainty of the nobody
who has the power over my mother's dreams,
over her days filled with quiet loneliness
and her tortured visits to the devil's den.

Next finger into her face.
Never.

Russian history on the tip of that finger.
Country of despots.
Country of slaves.
Whoever stands on top at the moment
gives the finger to the one below.

prairie apples

I called my father:
I went to buy an apple tree.
Can you imagine?

Your little daughter drove sixty miles
at breakneck speed along the prairies
as if she were a cowboy riding a horse.

Sky—so wide, land—so open, fields—so big
and me, at my wheel, wind in my face.
Can you imagine?

Me, the city girl from granite embankments
and palace squares. Me, the girl from the tiny
apartment, low wet skies over my head.

I went to buy an apple tree along a prairie road
apples with the old country taste.
Can you imagine?

He could not.

small things left behind

I used to like forest flowers (like my mother),
gentle inhabitants of the wild.
I had to bend down to see them
they were so small.

You often bought me teensy
tied-up bouquets
from the smiling *babushkas*
at the entrance to the metro.

Pale green hellebores in the late days of March
white lilies-of-the-valley at the beginning of May
and purple violets at the summer's entrance.

I kept petite jewels for months
dusty, dried and faded
in tiny, ceramic cream-jars.

We added more jars—life bloomed on
until we left.
The flowers went down the garbage chute
tumbled
from the ninth floor to the ground.
The jars went into the small crate
followed us into exile.

The jars now stand on a shelf in the basement.
For my first birthday on an alien planet
you brought me an orchid.
I saw a huge spider and started to cry.

Now I grow big, blousy flowers
lilies and roses,
irises and peonies,
bright oriental poppies.

No more small treasures, those too-gentle
flowers of first love
hidden from the eye.
To see them now I need glasses.

* *babushka*—Russian for grandmother

rational foot forward

We did not teach our kids to speak Russian. They learned a
few words. We kept an average Canadian household, had jobs,
paid taxes, spoke English at home and seldom cooked Russian
food. Friends of our kids always were surprised to find out
they had parents from Russia. We did not look it (your parents
are normal, your home smells different from homes of other
Russian immigrants, you eat normal food). They did not go to
our basement, smell the inconsolable loss seeping from the
unopened boxes packed with the books about St. Petersburg.
The boxes were shut, like I was. Taped to not let out the past.

Until ten years later. Our friend calls, he takes a group of ninth
graders to Leningrad, part of their Social Studies class. He asks
for some books. I used to be a city tour guide. My automatic
response—yes, yes. I hang up and panic. I should call back,
say no, no. My hands are too heavy to push even one button.
I am numb.

In the middle of night I creep to the basement. Open a box.
Stare and cry. A few hours crying before I open a book. A few
hours crying as I look at the pictures. A few hours crying as I
read some Russian words. A couple of days of mourning. By the
time my friend comes to pick up the books I appear calm, speak
in my studied English—the language I use to separate me from
that untranslatable entity, dripping the fog of Petersburg's
canals into the dusty boxes of the past.

I   do not look back.   I look ahead.   An average citizen.

discoveries

Pine nuts were called *kedrovie oreshki* and never hulled.
Kedr was the huge tree that grew in Siberia, only in Siberia.

Life was simple. Things existed in only one version.
There was one country and one truth for everybody.

Woe on you if you did not fit.

My discovery of the world began in Italy
We found pine trees full of nuts.

The nuts could be bought hulled.
I ate them by the mouthful.

The Siberian *kedr,* white pine, grows all over the globe.
I admire the one in my neighbour's big yard.

There are doubles and triples of everything.
I can call another country home, fit or not.

connections

How few are the things I can touch.
A silver spoon from the grandmother,
the cup bought the day my daughter was born,

a figurine from my mother's dresser.
Tiny, material links to a lost world
our family's life in each one.

How few are the things I can touch.
The piece of peach-coloured silk,
a striped wedding-gift towel,

an old, homemade summer dress.
The past I left behind,
the smell of my mother, her smile.

How few are the things I can touch.
Old letters in a seldom-opened box,
one brown album with black and white photographs:

my parents and brother look into my eyes
me as a child
before I knew myself.

How few are the things I can touch.
Memory holds the rest—faces, colours, sounds
and smells—smoke from a steamship floating by.

picking apples

I can still hear him, hear the voice of fresh snow creaking under my skates. I lean on a palisade fence. My grandpa teaches me how to skate. I am not sure whether he knows how, himself. But he holds my hands tight. We need only to go from the yard to the road where the snow is packed and my skates glide.

His comings and goings were always mysterious. I don't remember a train or a car. Just—when I came home, he was there. Sitting in the kitchen, drinking tea, talking to my mother and smiling at me with his charcoal eyes. He planted an apple seed to grow a tree. It grew! In front of the window! We checked on it every time he came.

He said, I will graft a good apple on it for you to pick when you grow up. I did not understand why a tree should grow on a tree. He never grafted it. He died that spring.

He came to visit one evening as usual, appearing from nowhere. This time in the kitchen, he and my mother looked at his blackened toe. Mother talked about the doctor. He joked with me. His foot got gangrene. The doctors decided to amputate. The operation failed. He was paralyzed and passed away in April, before Lenin's birthday. I remember sitting at my school's morning concert, not able to cry.

It took me many years to get to the place where my mother was born, where my grandfather built the house, looked after his land—fields of blue flax under the pale northern sky. An empty space where the house once stood, the big rock my mother hid under when she was a girl. They ran away when the *kolkhoz* came and the last cow was taken. Left—the house, the fields. Escaped—the hunger, the death, the Gulag.

I walked with my mother and aunt through the fields that used to be ours. Reluctantly we came to the garden—grandfather's pride overgrown with weeds. Large, dense apple trees full of small greenish apples. I bravely tried. Sour, wild—the dream apples he had never had a chance to graft. I planted an apple tree in my yard, in a different land, eons away. I bought the tree already grafted. I now pick apples.

* *kolkhoz*—Soviet collective farm

no answer to the questions not asked

i will never know
there is nobody left to ask
how the family survived
did somebody knock on a window
in the middle of the night
to whisper
it is time to run
an escape or a planned move
i will never know
children grew up
found in a cabbage patch
or delivered by a stork
large wings covering the dark shadows
no womb of the womb of the womb
to claim your heritage
hush, hush
shush, shush
let nobody ever hear
let nobody ever remember
just some light in my mother's eyes
that came from nowhere
and went
into nothing

Mayday flowers

My mother liked flowers. In the spring
I roamed the banks around a meandering
creek, nameless and narrow, filled

to the brim—tiny islands overgrown with wild
Mayday dreams. An annual pilgrimage the last
day of May, heady-smelling branches for our teachers

the parting gift, happiness—school finished
three months of freedom ahead. Glorious
symphony of sun, forest, river and beach.

Icy-cold water to jump in, boats to cross
the black, treacherous Neva (the daredevils
swam, some never made it to the shore).

Islands' cheerful sprays in our home.
We had only one vase—too tame for my wild
shade. Fragrance landed in shiny, aluminum

pails. Bucketfuls on the floor in each corner
of my mother's bedroom. Our tiny flat overwhelmed
by the intoxicating smell of my day, an oasis

in the drab Soviet life, mother—the bride
among flowering white. Her blissful smile,
face buried in airy blossoms, deep breaths

of spring. Her dark-copper head flamed
by the sun—a fire, bucket to bucket.
Her black, laughing eyes—a caress, corner

to corner, glowing at me. The happiness
islands. Her knowing voice meandered
like that jolly brook. Where have you been?

old dress

I did not say goodbye to my aunt.
Twilight, the bus, an old woman with the big
hips like mine in a white silky dress
with black flowers swirling on it. I liked
that dress. She made it herself, one for her
and one for my mother.
They often had identical dresses
bought double the fabric one of them liked.
One time the three of us had dresses from the same fabric
in different cuts. I did not find it
charming, never wore mine.
I have only one dress from her hands
the last one she sewed for me before I left.
It hangs in my closet like an amulet.
A wind from the past.
A voice from the dark.
The smell of her room.
Her hands slipping the dress
—her flesh and blood—onto me.
I hug it, since I cannot hug her.
The bus doors close.
She is inside, looking at me, and I stand on
the empty Leningrad road
hot, smoking August asphalt in my nostrils.

gold coins

My husband's grandfather suffered from a bad
memory. The CHEKA beat him and threw him
into a prison cell, so he would remember

where he hid his money. He remembered three
gold coins in the yard under the tree, they dug
out five coins and beat him to remember

where did he hide the three. He said
in the vegetable bed. They dug the vegetable bed
found two coins, beat him again to remember

the original three. He thought, they are next
to the raspberries. The CHEKA chopped
the raspberries, found a small bag of coins,

beat him more for the three. He finally
remembered, the three coins were under
the porch. This time they found

the three coins and let him out. He came home—
yard ruined—porch demolished—bones broken—
spirit crushed—hungry—poor.

* CHEKA—Soviet Secret Police, the precursor of the KGB, the name used from 1917 to 1922

you are my mother-in-law

1|

How do you pee in a cattle-train car filled with people
standing straight, tight like grass in the fields outside?
Endless stretch of suffering country getting colder

and colder as the train goes deeper and deeper into safety,
away from the bombs. You are lucky to be on this train
with hardly enough air to breathe. The one before was bombed,

obliterated, and you lay on the grass amongst the corpses
and screaming wounded, baby kicking in your womb.
Both your heart and the baby thump, thump, thump, louder

than the screams around, louder than the explosions
or screeching sounds of *Messers,* when they dive down to gun
people jumping from the burning train. Flames—the only light

in the night—smell of blood mixed with soil and gun powder.
A child's legs in brown sandals. Smell of death—life within you
rejects it. You retch and crawl, crawl, crawl.

* *Messers*—common name for the Messerschmitt, a German fighter plane during WWII

2|

How do you feed the baby in a small Siberian town
without food? Your mother, child, sister,
sister-in-law and niece—one cold, tiny room.

Hunger—your landlord. Rules the lot. Charges in flesh,
dignity, humiliation. The mandatory black dish
on the wall spits hourly—defeat, death, devastation.

Meagre belongings traded for food at a flea market,
where you are famous—name the asking and selling price
of your wares at once. Everything fair game, except

your husband's hankies, his shirts, that you hang
in your corner of the room, as if calling him to come back
from the lost. Lost in action—the official version

you got. Died, a letter from a well-meaning friend
details. Lie, you say, as you hug your baby, his shirts.
Don't cry and wait, wait, wait.

You get an accounting job. Nights are long. Nights
are cold. Sleepless, alone in the dark, you count—
seconds, minutes, days, weeks, months, years.

3|

How do you talk to a man returned from the dead?
His screams in the middle of the night, shadows of his family
perished in the Holocaust. Second child—the gift of your faith

smiles in the crib. Behind—wounds, POW camps,
German firing squad, escape, French Resistance,
repatriation, Gulag—all, but the KGB. He smokes

pack after pack, does not talk when he comes back
from their interrogations. Guilty of being alive, surviving,
fighting, getting the Order of the French Legion

that you only glanced at before he destroyed it—
the incrimination in a mad witch hunt.
Hundreds of thousands of returning POWs die in the Gulag.

Stalin—the *generalissimo*—honours his fighting men.
You wait for the knock on the door at night. You wait
as Mikhoels is murdered. You wait as the doctor's plot

is announced, as the cattle cars are prepared.
You hide your Jewish face riding the tram.
At Purim—Festival of Lots—Stalin dies. At work

you cry with the country, but at home—all smiles.
People who disappeared at night, millions and millions,
come back—those who are alive.

4|

How do you pay the police for your husband's life?
Soviet history loops—the government allows co-operatives
then forbids them, sends entrepreneurs to jail. Shoots some.

Your husband in hiding. Cities you never heard of. Family life
full of secrets. Daily, all there is to say—I don't know.
Whispered names, shadowed people, fear. Again, you count.

Husband back, daughter marries, grandchildren come,
son studies in Leningrad. Life shows you a rare smile,
then comes his first heart attack. Three more to follow.

You die and resurrect with each one. Cancer succeeds
where German bullets did not. You are now the witness. Lost. Split
in two. Your son leaves the country. You stay with your daughter.

my father tells me a story

I was not afraid. We were crossing the Dnepr. Bombs. Planes
fighting above our heads. Not enough of ours, *Messers* were
shooting people at will. The bridge packed—trucks, cars,
horse-drawn buggies, people on foot, children crying, soldiers
wounded, soldiers lost, all heads down. I looked at the river.
There was no water. I saw only fire. We moved slowly—dead
bodies, dead horses, abandoned lorries, dropped bags, torn
suitcases, bloodstained rags. My mother, sister, two younger
brothers on the *telega*. My father led the horse. My older brother
and me behind. The smell of burned flesh, my mother's
terrified face. I envisioned an acceptance letter from flying
school in our mailbox, my dream in my hands.

We crossed the bridge, all of us alive. Mother started to cry
as we moved into the forest. I ran to her, kissed her wet face
and turned back toward the bridge. She screamed, everybody
screamed, but they could not stop. I knew it, and there were
four other children to save. I waved, said as loudly as I could,
against the desolate mass of humanity running from hell,
I will leave with my flying school, and started to fight my way
back to the city.

There was no letter in our mailbox. Empty apartment. No food.
I turned on the light. I heard artillery noise, falling bombs. I
was not scared. The doorbell rang. My uncle. He was on his way
to the military barracks, to leave the next day. He saw a light,
came to check. Took me to the flying school that very moment.
Used his high rank. I left with the school in the morning.

Germans marched into the city the next day. Two cousins, my age, did not get out, were shot by the SS. I got to the Urals, studied, volunteered at the front. Became an artilleryman, not a pilot. Could not wait, had to fight back. I was not afraid.

wake-up call

Evening on Sunday
our supper is tea and the pies my mother baked
spending her day with the smell of the fried cabbage
apples and butter now melting on the hot crust

    They baked different pies when we were stationed in Estonia
    had such good milk
    after the hunger of war it was heaven
    to go to a market and buy food

    People did not like us much
    but were polite
    I didn't understand

    One summer morning I ran out of milk
    walked into town
    It was so quiet—strange

    I didn't meet anybody
    no women who used to stand at this corner and chat
    no children bumping into me, running late to school
    no grouchy old man who never acknowledged my nod
    Where did they hide?
    I ran to the bazaar along the sun-lit, empty streets

    The market deserted
    cleaned after closing
    for the next trading day that never came

I was so scared, hurried back to our barracks
passing one house after another
every door shut

Mother, where did they all go?
Who has done this?

perceptions

My husband, you were a shoemaker
in my dream. A small, old, iron mallet
in your hands, the tiny nails between
your teeth, you fixed my shoe. I only saw
the one, high-heeled, black patent leather
in your palm. If anything
you should've been a tailor
as your father suggested, thinking
a piece of bread would be always
in your hands.

Your father did not understand
a man like you, with two degrees, two
languages, a professional career.

But maybe it was not about you.
It was about him, his life,
his brush with death,
the piece of bread he dreamed about
in projector-driven barbed-wire nights
and the nightmare of days as a German POW.
When he escaped he ate rat, raw,
just skinned. His body refused meat
after the year of famine,
but he survived and fought in France.

As a man who had stood in front of a German
firing squad, your father did not circumcise you.
He wanted to give you a chance to hide.
He could not

His grey eyes
had averted the bullet: This one is pure Aryan,
said the SS officer, and pulled him
out of the death line. The Nazi arrogance,
superiority of judgement did not allow
the officer to pull down your father's pants.
Why should he?
He knew how Jews looked and smelled.

reflections

I catch a fish under a railroad bridge
in a small, cold brook. A fork is in my hand
eyes follow without break the small silver body in the water
and only the train above shakes my composure.

The dappled sun reflections still playing
on the surface of my memory like on the water.
The smell of mazut among rusted iron.
The twists of tiny fish on my raised fork.

I walk home along the railroad ties—the shortest way.
I sing, I feel myself a bird, alive,
alive without any knowledge of otherwise.
The cat ate my fish, its silver gone. The evening came.

I heard the brook dried out a while ago
and all the fish have left. I do not fly. I often
wonder if anybody found my tarnished fork
in the tall, wild grass that grew around.

hedgehog and turtle in Soviet Union

They were the usual fare
in Nature Corners
set up in every daycare
and elementary school
across the country.

A veritable army
of hedgehogs and turtles
marching across
one sixth of the planet.

The hard shells
and sharp needles
of our daily lives.

But rabbits were rare.
Rabbit was meat on a plate.
Most people preferred
the meat to the hunger
the semi-hunger
the memories of the hunger.

My father always
treated food like a miracle,
worried the miracle might end one day
corpses with empty eye sockets
might appear on the streets again.

Eat
he tells me
eat
eat
eat.
My chewing—the sound of life.

I know Germans, my grandfather said.
Cultured people. They treated us with respect
when they occupied our town in 1918—
much better than Whites or Reds
or Makhno bandits
who killed many Jews
and better than Soviets with their NKVD.

The German officer was billeted in my house.
The picture of civility,
he shared his food with us.
I am not going anywhere,
grandfather replied, when my father
came to evacuate the family
in the summer of 1941.

In that small Ukrainian town
nobody
had heard about the *Einsatzgruppen*
nobody
could envision the smoke of Auschwitz.

* NKVD—the KGB name in the 1930s

old photographs

My grandmother never laughs.

We sit in her small room
With a bed, a couch, a table and chairs
I am with her, but the room feels empty
Like somebody walked out and did not come back.
Whitewashed walls. Family photographs
In one large frame across from the couch.

People in the frame.
My grandpa, very young, my mother and aunt.
Young men I've never seen, with dark curly hair.
Grandma, who are they?
She looks past the picture, past me,
They are my Sasha and my Osip ...

Her voice is different, not the voice I know.
Not the voice she uses to talk to me.
I hug her. I am only seven, but I sense
They are the ones who did not come back.
I rush to the wall, touch the glass with my hands
Use my finger to outline their shapes.

Here, from the photographs on the wall
The life I do not know looks back at me
Full of uncles and aunts, cousins to play with—
A large family at the table, a happy, laughing grandmother.
Here, staring at me from the photographs on the wall
Is the meaning of war.

watching a military parade in the Soviet Union

The ritual starts days in advance. My mother is bent on getting provisions. There may be more food available at the stores before the holidays. Everybody expects they *vibrosyat* some smoked fish or sausage. You have to be watchful just like our army and border guards. We watch for food and they watch for our safety. The motto—clear sky above our heads. And a wounded generation repeats the words, toasting each other, To Peace, on Victory Day or Revolutionary Day, on International Labour Day—May First—and on any other occasion to toast. Twice-yearly military parades on Red Square—the guarantee of the clear sky above our heads.

My parents move a table to the edge of the room, almost to the hallway, so we can watch TV. Mother starts cooking festive breakfast early in the morning to be ready when the parade starts. She is never on time. She cooks so much. My father stands in the hallway, his eyes riveted to the TV, repeats parade commands with the announcer. Slices the bread at the same time as he names the marshals, present and past. By the time we sit down to eat, most of the infantry has passed through. The artillery and rockets come. Father greets *Katushas* with exclamations of pride, sometimes with tears in his eyes. The Germans were so afraid of them. They saved our lives. The war is fresh in his mind as if it just happened, the German bullet still lodged near his heart. The words of the motto are lodged there, too. I never saw my mother's brothers. One disappeared in action the first day of war, another, a captain, was killed in Poland in 1944. My mother and aunt found the grave, received letters and pictures from Poland.

The longing for peace is strong. Everybody I know, all around the country, was wounded on June 22, 1941, long before I was born. But I can hear the sirens, see the bombs falling in my sleep. In Leningrad I walk past a sign: *This side of the street is particularly dangerous during shelling*. The cemetery with more than a million dead in the nine-hundred-day siege. We learned to watch the skies.

On the TV screen, long-range missiles. The threatening, thunder-like noise fills Red Square, our room, and millions of rooms across the country. My father is proud. Ours are the best. Nobody can touch us while we have these. My peaceful, kind father who would not kill a fly. A wounded generation forever afraid. Lied into believing the deadly rockets can bring peace, a clear sky above our heads.

* *vibrosyat*—throw out, slang for short erratic appearance of consumer goods in stores

* *Katusha*—nickname for Russian multiple rocket launchers, first used in WWII

every May 9th of my childhood

1 | marching

The road from town to the graves is almost straight
looking back I do not see the end of the column
hundreds and hundreds of people
along a three-mile-long, boulder-paved alley
cut through the forest

The yearly homage to the fallen

We march

The military decorations glimmer
on the civilian jackets of old men and women
the wood around bursts with new life
green tender leaves unfurl
like the red flags we carry
white heads of the snowdrops nod

We march

2 | winds

Wrought-iron railing marks a modest military cemetery
a black metal monument tops the large mass grave
flanked by a few smaller ones
with some names on the obelisks
and the narrow, grey cobblestone pass
Stately fir trees stand guard

A young spring wind waves blood-coloured silk
like sails above a sea of solemn people
Sun mixes the resinous smell of needles
with the heat of the shining medals
alcohol from the men's mouths
women's Red Moscow scent

An earthy whiff of the graves' dirt
cuts the kids' smiles short

3 | voices

Eight of us, sixth graders, read poetry
Into the sun-filled air we send
words of death, heroism and hope
Old soldiers cry

What do they see through the mist of the tears?
Black smoke, burning Neva, earth blown up?
Or the smiles of the ones in the grave now?
Even they do not know the names of the dead.

What do they hear among the birds' spring chatter?
Artillery explosions, bombs falling, cracking of the machine-guns?
Or the screams and cries of the men silenced now
whose bodies are piled on one another in the burials around us?

4 | we look across the river to the left bank

These old men held the field across the river
the flat marshy area, no natural cover
a kilometre by a kilometre-and-a-half—
the size of a five kopek coin
grimly nicknamed by the soldiers "Nevsky pyatachok"
—Neva Bridgehead—the death trap
where the average lifespan was a few days
where the scarred terrain holds more human bones
and fragments of iron than particles of soil
where trees do not grow even today
where more than two hundred thousand died
on a tiny patch of land

Dug into mud for two years
crawling over the dead bodies of their friends
each fresh reinforcement pulverized
by continuous enemy fire
mess of blood, bones and flesh
No defence from the cold and snow
no wood, no trees to burn for fuel
water boiling in the blood-filled river
that breathes heavily behind their backs

"The one who did not see the Neva Bridgehead
did not see the war," is the soldiers' saying.

war harvest

The funeral does not attract reporters
the word "counsellor" is not in our country's vocabulary.
We cope the best we can.
Five girls in the dim. We make artificial flowers
for wreaths for the boy's graves.
My fingers too small to fold
faded red crepe paper into roses.
I wrap narrow strips of green
around thin metal wire for stems.

We do not talk about the boys.
Only about the mines
still in the forest twenty years after the war
or the grenades we throw into the fire.

How the boys misjudged the size of the blast
from the grenade, corroded as it emerged from the earth
in the spring just like the snowdrops, buttercups, wild leeks.

We gather death's harvest.
A grey-haired young woman walks behind the coffins
in a drizzling rain—
second time in three weeks.

She squeezes her husband's elbow
with thin fingers
green
from the bleeding flower stems.

bog cranberries best picked at the first frost

A thin crust of ice,
thin enough to crack with the tips of my fingers
and get to the deep-red cold berries
hiding under.
The ice will melt if we wait for the sun to warm up.
It is early October,
the sun has lost the impatience of summer,
my mother has not.

Mornings are best.
Cranberries nest among greenish moss in the bog.
Frozen dew like the glaze on a pie
she will bake from the glistening jewels
at the bottom of my huge bucket,
make the *Mors*
we will drink
through the dark barren squeeze of winter.

She organized the truck, leads
the once eager pickers, who now walk slowly
through a threadbare towel of morning fog
hanging loose on the pegs of trees.
I pick out my father's shape
at the edge of the marshy meadow.
No smile on his face.
Then he winks.

The two of us go hide in the truck.
No dreams of the pie,
no thoughts of the cold fruitless freeze will stop us.
A thermos of tea, a sausage sandwich.
He breathes on my frozen fingers.
Red tips in white clouds
like the cranberries my mother rolls in icing sugar
for the after-dinner sweets.

Grandma, I don't remember you

I only have the smell of tea to go by,
you never cooked a meal for me.
Yes, we had tea, from a samovar,
eggs in a bowl, a stack of *bliny*.
Sun warms your room through a dirty window,
melts the spring snow.
I understand now,
you did not recover from the blows—

loss of home,
fields of wind-singing blue flax,
to Stalin's collectivization plans,
the loss of both your sons
to Hitler's Barbarossa assault.
I thought you were ancient.
You were only slightly older
than I am now.

There is not a word of yours left,
only the soft E you used in my name,
only the way you treated a cold,
drinking straight vodka with tea.
With a small bottle, a red pepper on its label,
you sit at my aunt's table,
vodka in your glass, steaming tea in a cup,
sweat on your forehead.

Next morning aunt announces
you finished the vodka, the pot of tea,
slept the night, the cold is over.
I've told this story for years.
but I don't try your medicine.
Life has been kinder to me.
A soft landing in Canada after the loss of home.
Your treatment scares my soul.
The taste is too harsh.

* The Russian letter E is pronounced ye-

my cat Kilka

My cat, the only one I ever had, was saying goodbye to us.
He followed me and my mother along the streets, and crossed
a large, barren patch of land on our way to the train station.

We moved, he moved.
We stopped, he stopped.

We boarded a train and he climbed up a huge tree by the platform
and meowed with such fright and despair in his cat's voice
that I was ready to forget my Black Sea dreams.

He will be fine, he'll go back,
                                        (my mother said)
        the neighbours will feed him.

The train departed, the cat s c r e a m e d his cat's lungs out.
I plugged my ears with my hands and could not wipe the tears.

I had a great vacation, a month with mother. Away
from the daily drag she was a different woman. Young,
laughter cupped in her kind hands—eyes smiled, feet danced.

The cat was forgotten while we swam, suntanned
and took a boat to cruise the harbour in the night.
Turned out the cat was desperate without us, refused to eat

even the favourites
put into his own bowl,
in his own kitchen corner of our apartment.

The cat knew his home was deserted. The four of us
were on different trips, my father on business,
my brother visiting his friend.

Father came back first, a week later, and saved the cat.
But not for long. He was picked up by a team from Pavlov's
Research Institute while running his usual cat's errands.

He was not home in the evening. The streets were filled
with stories about a truck full of doomed cats and dogs.
My father went to Pavlov's gates.

It was no good.   The cat was lost.

Life was cruel to people, who would be sorry for the cat?

I still remember him, his funny name—
something like Russian-style anchovies,
that little salty fish he liked.

unravelling

1|

I have never been to Tashkent
no memories of the devastating earthquake and the deaths.
I remember the bazaars
the mounds of famed dry fruit—*uruck*
the smells—large green Asiatic melons and orange persimmons.
I remember the aroma of a well-cooked Uzbek pilaf.

Where do my memories come from?

2|

Maybe from the old Soviet movies
I saw as a child.
One of my favourites—*Hodja Nasredin*
A central Asian folk hero. I see him
move through the noisy bazaar on his donkey.
Take a stand for the people.
Argue with the emir.
Cook a thick soup out of water.
Teach the donkey to talk.
Cheat the rich out of their money
and give to the poor, always laughing ...

Oh yes, that's the bazaar.

3|

During the late sixties my upstairs neighbour
babushka Kurochkina
went with the sacks of our old clothes
to Tashkent's flea markets to trade for *uruck*.

We had clothes in those semi-hungry years
they had *uruck*—dried apricots
too prosaic a name for the smells of an exotic land
the dusty, noisy bazaars
the bright colours of central Asia
the long and exhausting trip
a rare piece of southern bounty in the deprived northern winter.

No, no, we called our apricots their Uzbek name—*uruck.*
We made lots of compotes,
the treat with a heavenly smell
a thick amber liquid to drink
a soft fruit to eat, and the pits.

The pits were cleaned
virtually polished.
I sat with my friends on the upstairs landing
in our apartment building
cracking the pits with an old, blackened hammer
picking the treasured kernels to eat.
Babushka Kurochkina slightly opened
her door to give us a few more ...

Oh yes, that's the mountains of dry fruit
that's the *uruck.*

4|

The big, green aromatic melons from Scheherazade's tales
dazzled like the treasures from Aladdin's cave
displayed in a vibrant, fabric-lined basket
an unaffordable delight for most Soviets
sold occasionally in Leningrad
at the best farmers' market.

Big, round-faced, narrow-eyed men
in bright Asian *tubiteikas* and colourful, cotton-wool *chalats*.
Fat fingers counted every kopek we gave
more than the weekly salary of my accountant-mother.
My parents looked at each other
decided to buy.
We kids had never tasted anything like it before.
They spoiled us rotten.

Oh, yes, that's the melon smell.

* *tubiteika*—An Uzbek hat, like a skullcap, embroidered in bright patterns

* *chalat*—Traditional Uzbek clothing, like a long housecoat in bright patterns

5|

The Uzbek pilaf—an exotic party dish in Soviet homes
was cooked in a heavy, cast iron pot with a rounded bottom—*kazan*.
The shortage of rice, the unavailability of lamb
the unattainable central Asian red pepper
one had to be a *Hodja Nasredin* to conjure the famed aroma.

My mother turned into an expert pilaf-maker
thanks to sporadic lessons during the visits
of my father's photographer friend.
He disappeared during the early sixties
when the government cracked down
on previously-allowed small private co-operatives.

Many aspiring entrepreneurs went to jail.
Many were shot.
His old-fashioned wooden camera stayed behind.
We kids played with it.
Nobody ever mentioned his name ...

Oh yes, that's the aroma of pilaf.

6|

The bright orange persimmons came from the parcels
my uncle sent from Andizhan, near Tashkent
where my cousins studied piano at the conservatory.
The parcels smelled like the south, sunny and fruity.

I thought their life must be somewhat better—
easier without the snow and cold.
My cousin came for a short visit
to see the wonders of St. Petersburg.

She told me how her hands hurt.
She could hardly play her piano.
They were sent every year to hand-pick cotton
in the vast Uzbekistan fields.

Bare hands, bugs, heat, constant bending, a heavy sack.
I understood—
it was not any better than us being sent
to dig potatoes out of the cold Leningrad mud.

After all, the whole country was
one big Gulag camp.
Different types of slave labour
and the guards in each place ...

Oh yes, that's the persimmons.

recurring dream

I am on a plane   walk down the aisle
All of a sudden the pilot announces
We are turning back
We have to land in Leningrad
I run to the cockpit
beat on the door

Again on a plane   the pilot announces
The plane has malfunctioned
We are landing in the USSR
I jump from my seat   run to the exit
I beat on the door
try to open the latch

Sometimes the plane is white   sometimes black
I smash the window
I grab a parachute
One thing always remains the same
The terrible panic   hopelessness
Fear and horror spreads inside

I scream and wake up   wet   shaken   terrified
I see the ceiling   it is stippled
Not Russia   not Leningrad
I dare to turn my head and look around
I am in my bedroom   at home   in Canada
I   have   escaped

choice

We made the choice by measuring distance
by the Soviet tanks' speed.
They rolled into Prague overnight.
The Seine's banks were not higher than the Vltava's.
We crossed the ocean.

I left the crowded streets
where I walked as part of the others
the imposing classical architecture that fit my small size
the moist air that smelled of thousands of years
of my people's wanderings.

Here among human-sized houses
I feel insignificant.
Here on wide streets I am conscious
of my loneliness.
Here everything is new and my past disappears.
Open spaces let me dump my shadows.
Easy to reinvent my life.
To forget who I am.

homesickness snapshot

Fifteen years after we left, my husband
visited there and he took a picture. Dirty
robin's egg blue walls of the old

crumbling building, dirty white of the trim
around each window frame, grimy
columns in corners, a roof in dirty grey.

It is November, dirty slush outside, mix
of melting white snow and brown earth
under the feet of my family in front

of the building entrance. Neighbour's windows
look at me. My mother smiles into the camera
in the black coat we bought for her here

my brother looking so much older than the last
time I saw him, my father in the back, my sister-in-law,
the nephew I have never met, my niece. It is November

the sky dirty blue-grey just the way I remember
as I look at the photo's date—fifteen years ago
in the middle of their absence in my life.

linden honey

At the height of *perestroika*
my mother comes for a visit.
She sits in my kitchen, holds me on her knees.
I try to be as light as a newborn baby.
She pats my head, runs her hand over my hair
      Koshechka, she says (Little Cat)
her caressing voice full of love.
I am well over thirty and have two kids.

I have brought home a few jars of honey
to please her and show off my life.
I open the first jar. Light amber colour, Tupelo.
She inhales—
      Oh, heavenly, what is it?
I say, Tupelo is a tree, it grows in Florida.
      Florida ...? How can you get honey from that far?

Next the small, ball-shaped jar of orange-blossom nectar.
An exotic smell with a hint of unknown flower gardens.
      Where does it come from? I never saw oranges grow.
California, I say
      California ... she repeats
      must be nice ... orange trees ...
Her dreamy voice drifts away into distant lands.

The last jar is my prize—
the yellow sun of the linden honey.
>
>   Mom, you told me about the linden honey of your childhood.
>   I never had a chance to try it back in the old country
>   and here it is, the taste of your home in this jar.

She takes the jar, looks at it.
>   Linden honey!
she says with surprise and a childish delight.
The magical moment
a gift never meant to be—
the miracle performed by Gorbachev.

She opens the jar like the door to her vanished home.
I study her face. I want her to be happy. I want her to know:
I live in a place were you can just go and buy   Linden Honey.
I want her to understand: I had to leave her, come to this country.
My kids ... they can have linden honey or any other, if they choose.

She smells, carefully, as if her life might escape from the jar.
She smiles at me. I see in her eyes: you did right.
She takes a deep breath
>   It smells just like I remember.
>   My father considered linden the best.
>   We had a few beehives around ...

The family story I didn't know begins.

I forgot my coat when I moved
into a different rented room in the spring.
I searched my old haunt in the fall when I got cold.
The space by the door was empty and silent
the hook did not talk.
I guessed—my coat, like Gogol's, went for a stroll
along noisy Nevsky from the corner of Hertzen Street
to the Moscow Train Station.
Admired the colonnade of Kazansky Cathedral
dropped in at the Writer's Bookstore
walked into the Eliseevsky grocery
and maybe even bought
two hundred grams of bologna sausage
a hundred of butter and one just-baked baton
the evening meal for three young girls.
It stopped in front of the large window
filled with Scheherazade's sweets
took a deep breath—no money
for the thousand-and-one-nights-dreams of baklava,
halvah, icing-sugar-white shakerbura.
We never met, my coat and I.
The footprints of its folds lost in the metro.

Some days when the sky turns
the shade of Petersburg grey
with some whites and some lilacs
mixed together with steel
when the clouds drip sadness and longing
I can feel almost at home.

I open the window and see my coat
flying like the cow from Chagall's painting.
Black sleeves filled with the young salty winds
buttons like cow's eyes
look around in wonder at the world.
Pockets full of books and a baton.
And I feel, I'm strolling along Nevsky
my hands in its sleeves
Baltic salt on my lips.

I don't put sugar in my tea

I drink my tea in the morning
blackcurrant jam on my bread.
I say to my aunt
    This is the first year I've harvested blackcurrants.
    This time I got there before the birds.
    My bushes are young.
    Will they produce more when they grow older?
    Tell me, because you know.

I turn to my mother
    This intense, home-tasting blackcurrant jam
    almost like yours was
    but I like my currants cooked
    not ground raw.
    I don't need a winter's supply of vitamins from this jar,
    just the taste ...

Empty room. No answer.
Silence drips from the walls into my cup.
The only sound—my teaspoon
on porcelain.

mirage

Grey day today. Skies cry since morning
drops of rain—tears of earth. Is it the dawn
of spring or the twilight of fall?

House—a big, open umbrella. My ambiguity
hides inside, well protected by solid walls
and the ceiling. Is life real or not?

Mystic peacock, candy-pink colour
in a magical Turkish garden of gold
on my wall. Under glass—the masked

figurines. Are they reminders of Venice
or St. Petersburg? Yellow walls of an undefined shade
quiver under the diffused light of rain.

Scheherazade palaces—a fairytale world
of luminous cups, shimmering, reflected
in a prism of angled mirrors.

Sara Mingardo sings Vivaldi's
Nisi Dominus. Voice rises and falls.
Music fills the emptiness of doubt.

reunion

How do you talk to grandchildren
who do not speak Russian?
Your granddaughter, red carnations in her hands
excited to have a grandmother at last.

Little boy peeks from behind his mother's knees.
He has his grandfather's name.
You are in a wheelchair, your son behind.
The flight has been exhausting, you only nod.

The flat land from a car window
foreign to your eyes   not home.
The city landscaped in English
numbered streets and cars, no people.

The green-grey room in the family house
a dusty-rose window into the unknown.
A world filled with the loss of everything you know
only an old housecoat for comfort.

You called me one morning, a year later
proud of your newest accomplishment—
cleared a mixed-up bill at Safeway
explained—in English—got money back.

You chuckled. First time I heard you laugh.
Did you find some peace among the grass
growing straight and tight in the vast stretches of prairie?
Some small happiness?

I do not know. That winter you died.

collapse

Nobody expected it
not the CIA with a budget in billions, nor MI6
nor Gorbachev, the hero of the day.
Not ordinary people. Not I.

You talked about the Mongols' three hundred-year yoke.
Who could have imagined
that the evil would go with the stroke of a hand
of a pen on paper?

Blood rivers did not flow.
Hungry corpses did not appear.
The miracle, fairytale.
In the year 1991 the giant collapsed.

Had feet of clay.
Turned out to be not the Colossus of Rhodes
lighting mankind's future
but the golem with a devil's gleaming eyes.

Came to life, ate millions and broke
hitting the dust from which it came.
The monster gone, people orphaned
lost in the lies told for generations

waking up one morning—the future gone
the past erased.
White becomes black, black becomes white
mixes into the grey of daily struggles

on unknown terrain, full of holes
instead of victor's marches.
I hear a low, monotonous sound
the lament of stolen lives.

seta naturale is the natural silk

We could not take our money with us. After paying the state
to become stateless we converted whatever was left into sellable
goods. Months before leaving we embarked on a chase for the
special items, objects convertible into cash at the end of our
unpredictable journey. Silk was one of the best. Flat, light.
It could fetch a good price—the perfect immigrant friend.
My mother scooped up a prize—a few metres of pure peach-
coloured silk. A romantic name, *Crêpe de Chine*. She brought it
to me proudly, like a dowry. The colour took my breath away.
I sighed at the silk. I had never imagined I could touch
something so luxurious.

The first months in Italy I resisted selling it. Kept saying,
later, there is still time. I went on a small tour organized by
the immigrants, silk with me. Spellbinding trip, Medici's
Florence, Venice's mirage, shell of Siena, Pisa's white grace.
After getting dazed on top of the world's most crooked landmark
our guide gave us half an hour—there is a small market on the
right side of the tower to sell our wares. I ran to the bus. Got my
silk. Spread it on my hands and shouted in my loudest voice—
seta naturale, seta naturale—hoping nobody would come. A few
women came, admired the colour, touched the texture, asked
how much. I looked at the silk. Saw my home, my mother.
Saw the peach colour on me. I counted our money, how long
it would last. Asked for a price, so high, I could not believe my
own words. One woman wanted it, bargained hard. I stopped
understanding Italian, repeated the same number like a badly
trained parrot. She got angry and left. A friend wanted to help

me, to stop the woman, to translate. I repeated, I will sell it only for that price. My life is worth something! The bus honked. I hugged my peach silk—my closest friend, almost lost.

I brought the silk to Canada. It lingered on my shelves, moving with me from place to place, the smile of my mother in its glossy folds. I picked up sewing, repeated my aunt's expert movements. Trained my hands. Years of watching her flowed into my fingers. Her spirit guided my pace, the noise of the sewing machine—her voice. I made evening pants and a top. The peach colour turned heads. Now it hangs in my closet, an old friend from the past. I check on it once in a while. I pat it. It's alive—from the time my mother was here, walking the earth, giving me this peach-coloured river, now flowing like Lethe between the two of us.

nebulous

Have you ever heard
your soul screaming at night?
I don't hear mine. I sleep.
I don't know where my soul goes
who it trusts.

Our only connections are dreams.
The glimmer of light in a yellow window
a sea of white mayday petals on a brown floor
puddles of melted snow under red rubber boots
a bus on Leningrad's August asphalt, ochre buildings in sight

and a moving tarmac at a grey airport
and a whisper—don't leave—
in my mother's voice.
My father's hand reaches for me
across the steel lake of the night.

I wake up, the world around me
palpable and sharp.
But sometimes, out of the corner of my eye
I see some transparent, flickering shadow
some strangely twisted mouth suspended in air.

striped cake

Up in the dark autumn sky
there is the planet I left behind.
A little dot on the arch of heaven,
like any other, indistinguishable from the rest.
Which one is mine?
The one with the birthday cake in the middle,
with candles my mother lights.
The striped birthday cake she has baked for me,
white layers for the day
black for the night.
Buttercream oozing its angelic origin
smelling of vanilla, like my mother's love.

Please give me a piece now.
White for happiness,
black for despair.
Have you always known I would have to leave?
Who has the happiness?
Who has the despair?
I live them both,
juggling all these long years,
the happiness of being
the despair of being apart.

Buttercream oozing,
now—your tears.
They are mixing with mine
as I bake the striped black and white cake in my kitchen.

Black is the earth in your grave,
white is the stone I put on it.
Send me some message from our planet,
tell me how to make buttercream once again.

innocents in the Soviet Union

There are people who hear
neither the cries of victims
nor the endless lies.
The lives they live are mere existence
they are deaf to the beat of time.

They dig comfortable holes in the shit-filled gutters
protect their turf by refusing to see
how they march on the corpses of millions of people.

They could have found out
the human cost of the communist nirvana.
They do not want to know,
jealously preserving the lies of their edifice.

There is danger in knowing.

I want to go home. I don't know where.
My kids have homing devices and come
despite the arguments and battles

we still fight. I am their home. But I lost
mine. I cannot go back. There is no place
for me to land, except in memories

and on YouTube, where thousands of exiles
like me dream golden images of childhood
and youth in a ruthless country. The images

are true—the songs, the poems, the buildings
the smiles, the laughs. The evil is hidden
as it has always been. Two parallels that never met

until I learned about Lobachevski and lost
the happy smile of a nirvana builder. Where
do I long to go? My country dissolved.

Four dreaded letters, USSR, faded
into history. My city got its name back.
Justice served. Somehow my loss

doubled, two words to pronounce
instead of one. I want to go home
so much that I do not talk. I am too late.

there is an empty space where I've been sitting

From time to time I say
It's time to go
From time to time I see
my city in dreams
From time to time I feel
a wind from the Baltic on my cheek

But something holds me
It used to be my fear
I was afraid to be anywhere
near the Empire
And now, years later,
what holds me from the trip?

What holds me
from sitting on the bench
in Pushkin's park
and looking at the lake and the Chesmen column?
I still remember
how I got up from it the last time

Maybe because
I said *proschai*—goodbye
and meant the word
said never—*nikogda*
and the sound got absorbed into my life
Maybe,   maybe

From time to time I realize
the place I long for has disappeared
the bench is rotten
the city has changed its name
From time to time I understand
I can't return to nowhere.

an outsider

1 | i am not here

i do not know where i live
a house on a street
a city by the river
cold brown water swirls north
past me

a country on the map
i speak a language
not mine
walk streets
familiar from the years flown by

my heart is silent
i float like a chip of wood
twirled
by the whirlpools of the river
far from its birthing log

2 | what's left

the rain's limp tapping on my roof
like cotton balls
soft
fluffy
cushy
without substance

drop a fistful of these balls on the floor
there will be no sound
no complaint
from being stuffed in a jar
shape changed
by crushing

squash one between the fingers
what's left is so thin
flat
lame
unrecognizable
a shadow of a former self

3 | dry weather

I hide among my books
check the weather on the screen.
What city am I in?
The weather network can move me any place
the planet at the tips of my small fingers
One click and I can see
rain in St. Petersburg
the fires around Moscow
and floods in Manitoba
I can be in Rome
or Paris
anywhere
Reality I cannot touch
the rains that do not fall
in my dry city

4 | that moss

I step on moss in my back yard
soft cushion of light green
between my beds
Unwelcome guest
a foreigner I did not plant
persists
grows without roots
on bare crushed red shale
The outsider
confined by wood and concrete
for years
Still an alien

5 | lost reality

Today I drink Russian Caravan
a smoky smell to imitate
the leather bags of camel trains
a mystery of Russia

My mother drank tea from India
three elephants on neon yellow
a small thick-paper box
thin silver foil inside

There are four of them
my two uncles, my father, their old friend.
I listen.
        Remember how cousin Yonia
        did not make it out of the city in time.
Grey heads shake. It's all fresh.
Mara's voice
        What about Rakheel
        she was saved—don't you remember
        that Russian hooligan, Kostia—
        how he ran after the column
        with a bunch of kids
        and when the Germans started to shoot
        he screamed
            Rakheel, duck, don't wait, Rakheel, fall
        She did, not from the bullets or from being smart,
        just from the animal fright—
        she was only a girl.
        That night Kostia crawled
        to the ravine, to the hole
        where the bodies fell
        on top of each other, all as one
        and he dug, in the bodies, as in the earth.
        Rakheel was alive.
        He carried her out, he was strong.
        To his mother Kostia said
        One word about Rakheel and I'll kill you.
        Such a hooligan.

Yes, she survived
hidden in his room, under a bed.

I ask if he is honoured? at Yad Vashem?

Oh no, Kostia died shortly after the war from TB
and in the Soviet Union we did not talk.

Mara stops
short of breath (she is eighty-five)
she has run her part of the relay.

Four pairs of eyes look at me. In the gripping silence I hear
Rakheel, duck, don't wait, Rakheel, fall

amnesia

for Alla Tumanov

The generation in the know, like the Holocaust survivors, dying out.
The youngest ones, sent to Siberia in the last wave of terror
before Stalin's death are now well into the grey-hair years.
They told their horror stories, wrote books about the atrocities.
The revelations did not change the country. The testimonies
came like mosquito bites. Lost in the vultures' frenzy—feeding
on the ruins of the Empire. The ordinary birds consumed by
daily struggles for survival amidst the collapsing edifice of the
collective dreams, turned deaf to the tales of prisons, deaths
and lies—the corporeal foundation for those elusive dreams.
The millions who disappeared into the night stood as timeless
shadows, once more denied rising with the long-awaited dawn.
The truth of light did not illuminate the darkness of the past.
The soul-searching did not happen.

By now many are nostalgic about the good old days when
the state took care of their meagre daily rations. They do not
ask, what was the price? My friend, who spent five years in
the Gulag (lost three of her young friends to bullets in the
Lubyanka's blood-stained basement) worries. The history
textbooks have been rewritten again, Stalin's portraits appear
more and more, and his descendant applies to court to sue a
newspaper for calling his grandfather "the murderer." The
grandson claims that Stalin did not kill a single person, there is
no signature of his on any order to kill the millions buried in the
communal graves across the country, still hidden from our eyes.

In Moscow there is a park, a tourist destination, old statues from the Soviet times. Dzerzhinsky, Lenin, Brezhnev, in bronze and marble, line the alleys. Dethroned from their solid pedestals in the first wave of liberation's excitement. The *generations after* stroll to ponder the country's past. What do they think? The massive figures, cracked and crumbling, are imposing in their frozen postures, with gazes fixed.

talking to an old photo album

I ask
Where are you?
Silence answers me
Look at you in this photograph
middle-aged
standing by the tiled wall near the stove
in the fur hat that I remember
On the same page, I am three years old
and you are the young mother
My granddaughter will soon catch up with me

Where are you?
Only the sounds of the white stones
little rocks on your grave
I have not been at the cemetery
for five years
the last time I waited and waited
you did not talk

The sky that I see
is wider and higher
the dryness here you would not like
I call this place home
thanking the land
for rolling
a carpet of prairie for me

Where are you?
I search in the grass
dry like tears
long like the past
that has caught up with me
Life that has parted us is over
and I can't explain to my children
Why did I leave? Why forever?
It looks quite ok in the old photographs
and the movies
I sit in front of the tv screen
and my tears don't dry
the prairies be damned

On this page
I am so small I don't know you
I don't know you on the next page
Have I ever known you?
We did not have a relationship as adults
when I grew up
I left
and remained your perpetual child

On the next page we pose together
fit into one frame for a moment
Look at my happy face
I did not know
that after parting
we would not live in the same frame
we age on different sides of the planet
On mine I learned
the colour of your eyes in the black and white photograph
has no name
and your smell is the smell of the dusty paper

how scared I am to turn the page

Where are you?
Does land keep bodies?
Do souls fly?
That dress you wear
that sepia-coloured embroidery
you do not smile
You do not smile in these old pictures
and I don't remember the real life
just the smell of your cabbage rolls
your White Lilac perfume
and sometimes your voice
as you tell me to sweep the floor

acknowledgments

acknowledgements

"Edmonton founded 1980" and "homesickness snapshot" were previously published in *Home and Away: Alberta's Finest Poets Muse on the Meaning of Home* (House of Blue Skies, 2009). "silence" was previously published in *Poetica Magazine*.

My deepest thanks to Pierrette Requier, the first listener of most of the poems in the book, for her gentle mentoring of my poetic voice, continuous encouragement, trust and support.

Thank you to Betsy Warland and Harold Rhenisch for their advice on earlier drafts of the book.

I am grateful to Al Moritz for his invaluable help in shaping the present version of my book, to Deborah Lawson for minding my "A"s and "The"s, and to Alice Major and Yukari Meldrum for their treasured friendship and unfailing support.

I owe a depth of gratitude to my editor Peter Midgley at the University of Alberta Press for his insights into my poetry, his understanding and encouragement.

This book would not be possible without unwavering love, faith and support of my husband Mark Zeltserman. To you is my eternal gratitude and love.

Other Titles from The University of Alberta Press

Man in Blue Pyjamas

A Prison Memoir

JALAL BARZANJI

SABAH A. SALIH, *Translator*

JOHN RALSTON SAUL, *Foreword*

288 pages | 34 B&W photographs, translator's preface,
   foreword, map

Wayfarer Series

978–0–88864–536–4 | $24.95 (T) paper

978–0–88864–611–8 | $19.99 (T) EPUB

978–0–88864–526–5 | $19.99 (T) Amazon Kindle

978–0–88864–784–9 | $19.99 (T) PDF

Memoir/Human Rights/Kurdistan

Dreaming of Elsewhere

Observations on Home

ESI EDUGYAN

MARINA ENDICOTT, *Introduction*

56 pages | Introduction, liminaire/foreword

Copublished with Canadian Literature Centre/
   Centre de littérature canadienne

Henry Kreisel Memorial Lecture Series

978–0–88864–821–1 | $10.95 (T) paper

978–0–88864–836–5 | $8.99 (T) EPUB

978–0–88864–837–2 | $8.99 (T) Amazon Kindle

978–0–88864–838–9 | $8.99 (T) PDF

Canadian Literature/Essay

Bosnia

In the Footsteps of Gavrilo Princip

TONY FABIJANČIĆ

264 pages | 45 B&W photographs, maps, index

Wayfarer Series

978–0–88864–519–7 | $29.95 (T) paper

978–0–88864–753–5 | $23.99 (T) PDF

Travel Writing/Politics/World History